READING POWER

American Tycoons

Henry Ford

and the Automobile Industry

Lewis K. Parker

The Rosen Publishing Group's
PowerKids Press™
New York

Published in 2003 by The Rosen Publishing Group, Inc.
29 East 21st Street, New York, NY 10010

First Edition

Book Design: Daniel Hosek

Photo Credits: Cover, pp. 4, 5, 9 (top), 9 (bottom, detail of original photo), 14, 18, 20 (bottom), 21 from the Collections of Henry Ford Museum & Greenfield Village; pp. 7, 8, 10, 11, 12, 13, 15, 16, 17, 19 © AP/Wide World Photos; p. 20 (top) © Underwood & Underwood/Corbis

Library of Congress Cataloging-in-Publication Data

Parker, Lewis K.
Henry Ford and the automobile industry / Lewis K. Parker.
p. cm. — (American tycoons / Lewis K. Parker)
Summary: Introduces the life of Henry Ford, who is best known for his development of an automobile, the Model T, which was affordable partly due to his use of the first moving assembly line.
Includes bibliographical references and index.
ISBN 0-8239-6451-5 (lib. bdg.)
1. Ford, Henry, 1863-1947—Juvenile literature. 2. Ford Motor Company—History—Juvenile literature. 3. Automobile industry and trade—United States—Biography—Juvenile literature. [1. Ford, Henry, 1863-1947. 2. Ford Motor Company—History. 3. Industrialists. 4. Automobile industry and trade—Biography.] I. Title.
TL140.F6 P37 2003
338.7'6292'092—dc21

2002002926
Rev.

Contents

The Early Years

Henry Ford did not make the first automobile. However, he did succeed in making an automobile that the average American worker could afford.

Henry Ford was born on July 30, 1863, near Dearborn, Michigan.

Henry Ford was born on a farm in Michigan. His father wanted him to be a farmer. However, Ford liked working with machines better.

Henry Ford at three years old

Check It Out

In 1876, Ford received a watch for his thirteenth birthday. He learned to take it apart and put it together again. By the time he was fifteen, he could repair just about any watch.

When Ford was sixteen years old, he moved to Detroit, Michigan. There, he found a job working in a machine shop. He also worked at night, fixing watches.

> "Machines are to a mechanic what books are to a writer. He gets ideas from them, and if he has any brains he will apply those ideas."
>
> —Henry Ford

Ford learned a lot about machines and engines while working in machine shops.

Ford's Family

In 1888, Henry Ford married Clara Bryant. They had a son named Edsel. In his spare time, Ford started making a gas engine. He also started working on an automobile that would use the gas engine to run.

Henry Ford worked on his automobile in a small, brick shed behind his home.

Ford called his wife "The Believer" because she believed that he could build an automobile.

Edsel and Henry Ford

Ford's First Car

In 1891, Ford got a job as an engineer at a company owned by Thomas Edison. When he was not at his job, he kept working at home on his automobile. In 1896, Ford finished building his first automobile.

Henry Ford (left) met Thomas Edison (right) while working for Edison's company. The two men became great friends.

Check It Out

Ford's first automobile was too big to get out of the brick shed where he built it. Ford had to tear down one of the shed's walls to get the automobile out.

Ford called his first car the Quadricycle. It had four bicycle tires. It could go 20 miles an hour.

Ford's Automobile Company

In 1899, Ford left his job with Edison's company and tried to start his own company to make automobiles. Ford wanted to make cars that many people could afford. The first two companies that he started failed. Then, in 1903, he was successful in starting the Ford Motor Company in Detroit, Michigan.

Ford built several racing cars. In 1903, the Ford 999 set a record with a speed of 60 miles an hour.

In its first two years, the Ford Motor Company made about 3,500 cars.

In 1908, the Ford Motor Company started selling a car called the Model T. It was easy to drive and did not cost much money. Many people bought the Model T.

The Model T came only in black. It was nicknamed the "Tin Lizzie." Over the years, Ford lowered the price of the Model T from $950 to $290 so that more people could buy it.

Check It Out

At that time, most workers were paid $2.34 each day to build automobiles. Ford paid his workers $5 a day. Henry Ford wanted his workers to be able to buy his cars.

In 1913, Ford started using a moving assembly line in his factory. Workers stood in one spot and added pieces to each car as it went past them on a moving belt.

A Model T took more than 12 hours to build before Ford started to use the assembly line. Once the assembly line was used, a Model T could be built in 1 hour and 33 minutes!

By 1927, Ford had sold more than 15 million Model T cars. However, sales started falling because people wanted cars with more style. So, Ford stopped producing the Model T and began making the Model A.

Check It Out

In 1927, Ford opened the world's largest car factory. More than 80,000 people worked there. Everything used to make a car, from steel to rubber, was made in the factory.

Ford's automobiles had made it possible to work and travel farther from home. This changed the way Americans lived.

Henry Ford's son, Edsel (right), became president of the Ford Motor Company in 1919. However, Henry Ford (left) still owned and ran the company. When Edsel Ford died in 1943, Henry Ford took over as president again.

More Than Cars

Henry Ford did more than make cars. In 1918, he ran for senator in the state of Michigan, but lost. At one time, he owned a newspaper company. Ford also gave money to build several schools, a museum, and a hospital.

Henry Ford lost the race for senator by only a few votes.

Clara and Henry Ford visit a school they started in Georgia.

On April 7, 1947, Henry Ford died in Dearborn, Michigan. He had made about $1 billion from the automobile industry. That would be about $36 billion today. Ford was one of America's most successful tycoons. Henry Ford's work with the automobile changed life in America forever.

The Ford Motor Company made a car called the Edsel, named after Ford's son.

Time Line

July 30, 1863	1888	1893	1896
Henry Ford is born	Marries Clara Bryant	Son, Edsel, is born	Builds his first car

Ford worked hard his entire life to change and shape the automobile industry.

1903	1908	1913	1927	April 7, 1947
Starts the Ford Motor Company	Starts making the Model T	Starts using the assembly line	Stops making the Model T; produces the Model A	Henry Ford dies in Dearborn, Michigan

Glossary

assembly line (uh-**sehm**-blee **lyn**) a row of workers and machines along which work passes until a product is completely put together

engine (**ehn**-juhn) the motor that powers a machine

engineer (ehn-juh-**nihr**) a person who plans and builds things

industry (**ihn**-duh-stree) a kind of business that makes a particular product, usually in a factory

mechanic (muh-**kan**-ihk) a person who repairs machines

museum (myoo-**zee**-uhm) a place where objects are shown and studied

senator (**sehn**-uh-tuhr) a member of the United States Congress, which makes the laws of the country

tycoons (ty-**koonz**) businesspeople with a lot of wealth and power

Resources

Books

Henry Ford: Building Cars for Everyone
by Pat McCarthy
Enslow Publishers (2002)

Wheels of Time: A Biography of Henry Ford
by Catherine Gourley
Millbrook Press (1997)

Web Sites

Due to the changing nature of Internet links, PowerKids Press has developed an online list of Web sites related to the subjects of this book. This site is updated regularly. Please use this link to access the list:

http://www.powerkidslinks.com/aty/hfa/

Index

Word Count: 524

Note to Librarians, Teachers, and Parents

If reading is a challenge, Reading Power is a solution! Reading Power is perfect for readers who want high-interest subject matter at an accessible reading level. These fact-filled, photo-illustrated books are designed for readers who want straightforward vocabulary, engaging topics, and a manageable reading experience. With clear picture/text correspondence, leveled Reading Power books put the reader in charge. Now readers have the power to get the information they want and the skills they need in a user-friendly format.